pause
every day ●●●

An Hachette UK Company
www.hachette.co.uk

First published in Great Britain in 2018 by Aster,
an imprint of Octopus Publishing Group Ltd,
Carmelite House, 50 Victoria Embankment, London EC4Y 0DZ
www.octopusbooks.co.uk

ISBN 978-1-91202-353-0

A CIP catalogue record for this book is available from the British Library.

Printed and bound in China
10 9 8 7 6 5 4 3 2

Consultant Publisher Kate Adams
Art Director Yasia Williams-Leedham
Designer Sally Bond
Senior Editor Alex Stetter
Copy Editor Marion Paull
Production Manager Caroline Alberti

pause

every day •••

20 mindful practices for calm & clarity

Danielle Marchant

aster

Contents

Introduction

Life – a practice run

Pause is a philosophy that runs deep within me. The idea of the Pause is not about escaping but *being fully in* your everyday life. Most of us are not destined to spend our days in a mountain cave (although I'm sure this fantasy might sometimes appeal) and, despite the explosion of retreats on offer, it is not always a practical option to whisk yourself away from the responsibilities of everyday life, even for just a few days. While I believe wholeheartedly in the power of retreats, I appreciate they can seem a luxury in terms of either time or money or indeed both.

The idea of the Pause is an invitation to be more of who you are and encourage you to engage with the world around you, just as it is. Pause is a way of being that allows you to be more fully you.

This book offers a series of practices for you to explore. Some can be done regularly, even daily, and are perhaps more effective that way. Others are useful in a particular situation or circumstance. All of them, at one time or another over the past 20 years, have proved to be of service to me in my own life.

It is important not to treat this book as a set of demands, another list of tasks on your never-ending to-do list. Pause is gentler, kinder and more forgiving than that. These are ideas for you to play with, to arouse your curiosity and to accept or let go of as you choose.

Often, we think we should be farther ahead than we are. The critical voice in our head tells us we should have already learned that lesson and moved on. We think we're too slow in grasping all that we want to learn and forget that it will take a lifetime (and often many more) for the learning our soul desires to settle in. It can ease the pressure to know that we're all here to learn, in whatever time is needed.

The power of the Pause lies in its simplicity – after all, isn't life complicated enough? Remember, this isn't an instruction book, or a book of demands, but if you want to take the opportunity to Pause in everyday life, these simple practices will help you to do that.

If you are looking for a short cut (and let's be honest, who isn't?) you could begin by choosing one of the following ten Pause Practices and notice the impact it has on your life. Of course, there isn't really a short cut to life; it is meant to be lived fully and experienced in totality. Pause Practices are simply a way to help you with that.

As one teacher said: "Practise, practise, practise, until it becomes your practice."

Pause Practices

1. Walk slowly
2. Breathe deeply
3. Eat deliberately
4. Speak honestly
5. Spend prudently
6. Look softly
7. Relate kindly
8. Think freely
9. Love fully
10. Live purposefully

1

pause
for busy minds

How to focus a busy mind

Every day we are multitasking, whether we want to or not! Answering emails as we travel to work, stressing about multiple tasks that need to be completed throughout the day, checking phones while we make dinner and deal with homework. When multitasking becomes the norm, we can feel overwhelmed. The mind can start to race and be distracted, making it hard to focus on what needs to be done, and even though we are completely competent, completing even simple things can become difficult.

One way to help refocus your busy mind is by spiral breathing. This allows you to settle the feelings of being inundated by drawing your attention away from the busy thoughts in your mind. The practice of spiral breathing will help you to develop your concentration and focus.

Usually, one breath has two parts, an inhalation and an exhalation. Spiral breathing has four parts, each part lasting for the same amount of time. The four parts make one breath:

1. Inhale
2. Pause with the lungs full
3. Exhale
4. Pause with the lungs empty

The full process is outlined overleaf. Each part of the breath should take a count of six. If that's too much to begin with, reduce it to a count that feels comfortable to you. There's no rush. Breathe deeply and let it spiral slowly. Make these breaths the most focused but relaxing breaths you've experienced all day. Once you have practised spiral breathing, try to complete one small task from start to finish with total focus. Remember, we're not really meant to multitask all of the time!

Pause with spiral breathing

Time 10–15 minutes

Frequency As often as you can!

Location Find a place to sit, ideally a quiet corner at home where you won't be disturbed

Preparation

- Light a candle to begin. Tell yourself you are going to practise spiral breathing for a few minutes and that at this time nothing else is a priority.

- Sit comfortably and begin to focus on your regular breathing. Don't try to alter it at this stage, just breathe normally.

- Relax your body as you breathe, letting go of any tension. Close your eyes.

Exercise

- Take a deep breath in, allowing your breath to spiral up your spine for a count of six.

- Pause with full lungs for a count of six. Then as you exhale, let the breath naturally spiral back down your spine for a count of six.

- Pause with your lungs empty for a count of six.

- Try this again, inhaling and spiralling the breath up your spine, pausing and then exhaling and spiralling the breath down your spine, pausing again with your lungs empty.

- Repeat the four-part breath ten times. You can count the number of breaths on your fingers.

- When you have completed ten breaths, sit quietly with your eyes closed. Let yourself absorb the effects of the breathing and slowly return to your regular breathing.

- Try not to rush back into life after this Pause Practice, take your time. Go slowly, and explore what it is like to be more focused!

How to slow down your busy mind with one simple habit

This balanced-breathing exercise is designed to help you unwind in those moments when you feel under pressure. Use it to let go of stresses, strains and challenges and it will leave you feeling relaxed and light.

Pause with balanced breathing

Time Less than 5 minutes
Frequency Whenever your mind is busy
Location Anywhere – on the bus, at a meeting,
during yoga class

Preparation

• Turn your smartphone to silent.

Exercise

• Sit or stand comfortably, taking a moment to adjust your
body so you feel at ease. Give yourself permission to
pause, slow down and simply relax. There is nothing you
need to do. This is your time, just for you.

• For this exercise, you are going to breathe through your
nose only. To start, close your mouth and inhale through
your nose for a count of four, then exhale through your
nose for a count of four. Repeat the exercise ten times.

• Now let your breathing return to its normal rhythm
and notice how your mind and nervous system have
naturally calmed.

• Over time you can increase the count to six. As that
becomes easier, you can build to a count of eight if you
wish, but if you prefer to stay at four or six, that's OK, too
– whatever feels best for you.

pause
for calm

How to reduce anxiety and feel calm again

Anxiety is a normal response to situations that are new or challenging, but more and more people are experiencing anxiety on a day-to-day basis.

When this happens, as well as having to deal with the physical symptoms, such as shortness of breath, tension headaches or a churning stomach, it can be hard to think clearly. Simple decisions appear to be difficult or overwhelming. At the same time, they often seem more urgent than they actually are, and you end up feeling pressure to make a decision while not being able to see your options and possibilities clearly. This can leave you feeling more anxious and so the cycle builds.

To help with this, it is useful to get to know your own symptoms of anxiety. Do you have a headache when you're anxious? Does your heart rate increase? Do you notice that your body feels shakier? Do you experience tightness in your chest? What are your familiar signs of anxiety?

When you are anxious, your breath starts to constrict in the chest area, which makes it harder to breathe and increases your anxiety levels. This simple Pause Practice, utilizing abdominal breathing, will help calm you. You can practise it at any time and the good news is that no one else needs to know you're doing it!

Pause with abdominal breathing

———

Time 5 minutes
Frequency Whenever you feel anxious
Location Anywhere!

Preparation

• Identify your own triggers and signs of anxiety.

Exercise

• To begin, fully exhale for one breath to help reset your natural breathing pattern. Then take a deep breath in through your nose and down into your stomach. Breathe out gently through your mouth, as though you are blowing out a candle.

• This abdominal breath allows the tightness in your chest to begin to dissolve. Take as many as feels right. It might be three or five or ten or more. The trick is to keep going until you can feel your anxiety reducing and a sense of calmness returning.

• Let's try three breaths now. Take a deeper inhale through your mouth, letting the breath go down into your belly and then gently exhale through your mouth, just like blowing out a candle. Repeat twice more.

• Now let your breath return to its normal rhythm. As you settle, notice how you are feeling.

How to create more time when you feel squeezed

When your diary is bursting at the seams, you have to become smart at setting aside time for yourself. Otherwise, you are the last one to have your needs taken care of.

This Pause Practice requires advance planning. As you get into the habit of creating white space, it will become more natural and easier to do.

Pause with white space

———

Time 15–20 minutes
Frequency Weekly
Location At home or at work

Preparation

- You will need your online calendar or your diary
  and a pen.

Exercise

- At the end or the beginning of the week (whichever
  makes more sense to you), look at your calendar for
  the next four weeks. First, block out your meal times
  – schedule breakfast, lunch and dinner as white space
  on a daily basis. If this is new for you, or feels strange,
  just notice that and remember that you do need to eat
  every day! If you commute or have a daily school run,
  add that to your calendar as well to make sure the time is
  accounted for.

- Next, look at your business appointments and identify any that follow straight on from the previous one. For any meetings that are back to back, reduce the time allocated by 10 or 15 minutes. Make it a practice to schedule shorter meetings with white space between – you need time to digest and assimilate before absorbing more information.

- Now look at your personal appointments. Have you allowed enough travel time? Is anything double booked that needs to be cancelled? Have you prioritized the things that matter to you, such as going to the gym or a yoga class?

- Finally, look at your weekends. Have you left white space for doing nothing, allowed time to use as you please? If not, look ahead and plan it in. This is important – creating white space is about being as devoted to yourself and your needs as you are to others, because being devoted to others truly works only when you have been devoted to yourself.

3

pause
for vitality

How to re-energize when you're running on empty

Most of us experience times when we would like nothing more than to cosy up and indulge in a duvet day, but various commitments and responsibilities require us to keep going.

The challenge with this is that once your "energy tank" runs low, the body has to fight harder to stay in balance. The more you try to run on an empty tank, the more exhausted you become. We can probably do this occasionally – after all, the body is very resilient – but if you are repeatedly running on empty, not getting enough sleep, experiencing high stress and eating processed foods, over time your body will become weary, your hormones unbalanced and your qi (the vital life-force energy within all of us) will be depleted.

As well as taking care of your rest, nourishment and stress levels, you can support your system by cultivating the qi in your body. The next Pause Practice is taken from the traditional Chinese art of qigong. A simple but powerful practice, upholding heaven is perfect for raising qi (energy) in the body and helping you to feel re-energized.

Pause with upholding heaven

———

Time 10 minutes

Frequency As often as you like

Location At home or at the office. This practice
is particularly good performed barefoot in a park
or in the garden

Preparation

• Loosen any tight clothing or belt and, if possible, remove
  your shoes.

Exercise

• To begin, stand with your feet comfortably apart,
  keeping your arms at your sides and your eyes open.
  Focus on your breath. Inhale slowly through the nose,
  filling your belly with air. As you breathe in, raise your
  arms out to the sides and up above your head.

- As your hands meet above your head, exhale and interlock your fingers with your palms facing down.

- Inhale, rotating your hands, fingers still interlocked, so that your palms face the sky.

- Exhale. Look up at the back of your hands. Inhale and, if you can, inhale a little more, stretching upward as if you are wanting to push your hands up toward heaven. Keep focusing on your breath.

- Exhale while you let your arms float down to your sides. Keep exhaling, letting go of your tension. Relax your shoulders.

- Repeat this deep-breathing exercise at least five more times. Focus on your breathing, allowing your body to relax a little more each time you exhale.

How to release your back after screen time

If you spend a lot of time hunched over a screen – computer, laptop or phone – you may begin to notice the area in your upper back between your shoulder blades becoming stiff and tensed. This area of the spine is known as T3 and if it feels tight, you may benefit from mobilizing it. It can be a bit tricky to reach but the following exercises are designed to hit the spot. As well as doing these stretches, focus on your shoulders during the day, rolling them back so that the front of your chest becomes more open while you are sitting in front of, or poring over, a screen.

Pause with T3 spine stretches

Time 10–15 minutes
Frequency Daily as needed
Location At home or at work – you will need a
doorway or a wall for the third stretch

Preparation

- Loosen a tight belt or restrictive clothing and, if possible, remove your shoes.

- Stand with your legs hip-width apart. Take a moment to feel your feet on the floor and notice how your body feels as you simply stand.

- Inhale deeply and exhale gently. Repeat three times. Let your shoulders melt away from your ears with each breath.

- Gently move your right ear toward your right shoulder. Return to centre and then let your left ear drift toward your left shoulder. Repeat three times, increasing the stretch in your neck a little each time.

Pause with T3 spine stretches (continued)

Exercise

Stretch 1:

- Start from a standing position, feet hip-width apart. Place your hands on your hips. Inhale and lean backward, squeezing your shoulder blades together. Lift your chest and, if comfortable, lean your head backward.

- Exhale, tuck your tailbone under and round your back forward, collapsing your chest and tucking in your chin. Round your shoulders as much as you can.

- Repeat slowly five times.

Stretch 2:

- Take your arms behind you and clasp your hands together, interlocking your fingers.

- Raise your arms to a point that is comfortable, bracing your shoulder blades as you do so.

- Extend your head back, inhale and hold. Exhale and release.

- Repeat slowly five times.

- Stretch 3:

- Place your hands on either side of a doorway, or against a wall. Adjust your feet so they are farther back than your hips. Tilt your tailbone upward.

- Bend the elbows and move the chest forward. Push the T3 area forward and squeeze the shoulder blades together.

- Experiment with the height of your hands, and the tilt of your head until you find the most beneficial position for you.

- Straighten your arms, tuck your tailbone under and bring your chin to your chest.

- Once you have the most effective position for you, begin to coordinate the movement with your breath. Inhale forward and exhale backward.

- Repeat slowly five times.

4

pause
for perspective

How to get unstuck when you feel powerless

There are many different reasons why you may feel baffled and at a loss to know what to do. Perhaps you are stuck in a job, or a conflict, or a relationship or are nonplussed about a decision you need to make. That feeling can be immobilizing. You know something needs to change and that you need to act, but you feel paralysed.

Often feeling stuck is a signal of impending change, but we don't always realize this. Instead, we experience the inertia, which is usually frustrating. Sometimes, though, being stuck can be comfortable because deep down, we know that to act will require us to make a change that we don't really want.

This Pause Practice is a journal exercise that requires total honesty with yourself.

Pause with honest feeling

Time 30–40 minutes
Frequency Whenever you feel stuck
Location Outside in nature is good, but you can
do this wherever you choose

Preparation

- You will need a journal and a pen.

Exercise

- At the top of a clean left-hand page write the challenge,
  change or situation you are currently experiencing.

- Then write down all of your feelings associated with this
  challenge, one statement per line on the left-hand page
  only. You will be using the right-hand side to respond in
  a moment.

- If you need to write more than one page, continue on
  the next left-hand page. Likewise, for the following lists,
  use the left-hand page only, using a new line for each
  statement.

- Write down any thoughts you have, positive or negative, about the situation. Write as much as you can, going as deep as you can – don't hold back here!

- Now write down any thoughts or feelings you have about your life in relation to the change or challenge you are facing.

- Finally, write down any thoughts or feelings you have about anyone else who might be related to this situation.

- Now take a break. Get up, move around, go for a walk, dance. Do whatever feels best for you in this moment to move your body and when you come back, find another place to sit, if you can, to complete the exercise. This is called "breaking state" and is useful, particularly as you were just writing about being stuck!

- Now you are going to be an impartial witness who will read each of the statements and, on the right-hand side of the page, respond to them one at a time. The purpose is not to ignore the facts or try to make a bad situation seem better than it is. The purpose is to be real, honest, truthful and wise about what you see on the page. When you feel stuck, ask yourself what is really true. Know that your emotions are always real, but the thoughts that created them may not always be true.

Pause with honest feeling (continued)

- Keep working through until you reach the end, and then take some time to see what you have discovered. What new insights have emerged? Can you see what actions are important for you to take now?

- Finally, find a clean double page in your journal and head one side "Choices" and the other side "Chances". What choices can you make for yourself now? What chances (small risks) would you like to take? Write down as much as you can.

How to unstick a difficult relationship

We relate to people every day, either in person or virtually, so we all know that the nature of relationships is that they don't always run smoothly! Sometimes situations arise where there is conflict, at work with a boss, colleague, peer, team member or customer. At home, conflicts can arise with parents, partners, children, siblings or even friends.

When these conflicts occur, separation can follow, which in turn makes it hard to relate to the other person. Feeling wronged by another is painful, and often makes us want to defend our own position. This is natural, but in our defended place it becomes difficult to access compassion and empathy, for ourselves and for the other person or people. We can also lose connection to our inner wisdom and insight.

This Pause Practice provides an opportunity to stand back and see the situation through fresh eyes. It encourages empathy and enables you to think more flexibly and creatively again.

Note this exercise isn't about always seeing the good in another person. Sometimes that person has behaved in an unjust way. If this is the case, it needs to be acknowledged honestly in this practice; otherwise you will continue to feel wronged.

Pause with perceptual positions

Time 20–30 minutes

Frequency Whenever you have conflict
with another person

Location A quiet space at home or at the office
where you won't be disturbed

Preparation

- You will need three sheets of writing paper and a pen.

- Think about the person or situation that's troubling you.

- On one sheet write: *POSITION ONE: MYSELF.*

- On another sheet write: *POSITION TWO:* and add the
  name of the other person. For the sake of convenience,
  let's call him Joe.

- On the third sheet write: *POSITION THREE: OBSERVER.*

- Now place the first sheet of paper on the floor to
  represent you.

- Place the second sheet opposite the first, at a distance
  that feels right for you.

- Place the third sheet either to the left or right of the
  first two, creating a triangle.

Pause with perceptual positions (continued)

Exercise

- Once the sheets of paper are arranged on the floor, take a moment to step onto *POSITION ONE*. Think about Joe and look over to *POSITION TWO*. Imagine him standing there in front of you.

- Become aware of the thoughts and feelings that arise within you. Take your time to live the situation as though you are back in it right now. See what you see, hear what you hear and feel what you feel.

- When you are ready, step off *POSITION ONE* and shake your body to "break state".

- Now move over to *POSITION TWO* and look at *POSITION ONE*. Imagine yourself as Joe looking at you. See what he sees, hear what he hears and feel what he feels. Take your time. Let the awareness move through you.

- When you are ready, step off *POSITION TWO* and "break state".

- Now move to *POSITION THREE* and observe both Joe and yourself from a fresh perspective. Here you have access to higher wisdom and guidance. From this position as an objective observer you are able to see multiple perspectives and offer advice, suggestions and insight. Take your time as the objective observer. See what you see, hear what you hear, feel what you feel.

- When you are ready, step off *POSITION THREE* and give yourself a shake to "break state".

- Finally, return to *POSITION ONE*. Notice what it is like to return to this position. Be aware of your thoughts and feelings. Allow the insights from *POSITION THREE* to settle within you and be aware of how you feel toward Joe.

- When you are ready, step off *POSITION ONE* to complete the process.

5

pause
for clarity

How to stop overthinking

Clear thinking is a great asset but hard to achieve when your mind is racing at a hundred miles an hour. Meditation is one way to help you be more in charge. If you are new to this, or have struggled with it, a lovely breathing exercise, called bee breathing (*Brahmari pranayama*), can help you to slow your mind and calm your central nervous system, so that over time you will find it easier to meditate.

Bee breathing works well when your mind is in overload, because the sound you make is a distraction, and the mind loves a distraction! This practice works by blocking out the senses of sight and sound and creating an internal vibration by humming. The hum sounds like a bee buzzing, hence the name.

If you want to think more clearly, practise bee breathing regularly – it will really help.

Pause with bee breathing

Time 10 – 15 minutes

Frequency Daily if you like. This is a lovely
morning practice

Location A private place where you can be alone

Preparation

• Read this through in full before you begin.

• Find a place you can be alone for a few minutes and sit
in a comfortable position, with your back straight.

• Scan your body and notice how you are feeling.

Exercise

• Close your eyes, put your thumbs in your ears and use your forefingers gently to cover your eyes. The idea is to block out the senses of sight and sound for a few moments.

• Inhale, and on the exhale make a humming sound. Notice where your hum naturally comes from. For some people, it will rise from the chest, others will feel it come from the back of the throat. Let it resonate as your body intends.

• Repeat for ten breaths. You can vary the tone and speed of your hum as you like.

• Then, keeping your eyes closed, rub your hands together to generate some heat and place them over your face.

• Gently open your eyes and remove your hands.

• Scan your body again and notice how you feel.

How to connect to higher guidance

Entelechy is a word that Aristotle used to describe higher guidance and purpose. It assumes that all living things in nature already know what they will become, referred to as "the end within". For example, a grand oak tree is the entelechy of an acorn. Entelechy is encoded into every living thing and has a beginning, a middle and an end, which often leads back to a beginning in the cyclical nature of life.

This Pause Practice is designed to help you access your own innate understanding of your inner code, an opportunity for you to grow to know yourself. It is important to remember that you are not looking for the ultimate answer here, and that this is not a linear process. Rather, you are exploring your own inner map, which can be revisited at any time. The idea is that the more open you are to your inner map, the more creative are the choices you make.

You are going to write a letter to yourself. It is a particular type of letter, from your future self to your present self. Your future self will share with you wisdom about life, love and work as well as about your dreams, hopes, fears and beliefs. You'll discover what success really meant to you, how you touched other people's lives and the difference you were able to make.

Pause with entelechy

Time 30–40 minutes
Frequency Occasionally
Location A quiet place at home
where you won't be disturbed

Preparation

- Create a calming space. Light a candle or some incense if you like.

- Have your journal and a pen ready.

Exercise

• Settle down in your chosen quiet space and take some time to think about a point in the future when you will be nearing the end of your life. You might decide to use your 90th birthday, or a certain number of years from now. Let yourself immerse into your future self, see where you are and who is around you. When you feel connected and embodied into your future self, it is time to begin your letter.

• Start with "Dear" and insert your name. Let your future self write to you with kindness, compassion, wisdom, honesty and hope. Write for as long as you want, and allow yourself to feel deeply as you go along.

• When you have finished, take some quiet time to reflect on the words. When you feel ready (and this may be on another day), read back what you have written. You may want to ask a trusted friend or coach to witness your letter. You can write one of these letters to yourself annually, or more frequently if you want additional guidance.

6

pause
for gratitude

How to open your heart

The heart is vulnerable. We can experience
heartbreak, not just at the end of a relationship
or when someone dies, but at times when we are
treated unfairly, or when we watch the news and
see what is happening to humanity and our planet,
and we can even carry heartbreak and trauma from
childhood or previous lives.

As we experience this emotional turmoil, it's easy
to close the heart to protect it from hurt and further
pain, but this also reduces our capacity to give and
receive love and to feel gratitude. This Pause Practice
is a yin yoga asana (pose). Called melting heart
(*Anahatasana*), it is designed to help you gently
open your heart, without forcing it, so you can feel
gratitude again.

Yin yoga asanas are different from dynamic yoga
asanas, and are usually practised close to the floor.
The asanas are held for three to five minutes
and allow the fascia, which is the dense web of
connective tissue that surrounds our organs, muscles
and nerves, time to stretch and unwind. This
action begins to release trauma (either physical or
emotional) that is stored in the body.

Pause with melting heart

———

Time 10 minutes
Frequency As needed.
This could form a daily practice each morning
Location At home

Preparation

• Lay a yoga mat, blanket or folded towel on the floor.

• Wear something comfortable.

• Light a candle or some incense if you want to.

Exercise

- Sit on your mat for a couple of minutes before you begin and observe where you are today. Become aware of your breathing but don't try to change it.

- Come onto your hands and knees, and slowly walk your hands forward. Keep your hips above your knees and allow your chest to drop toward the floor. Still with hips above your knees, rest your forehead on the floor. If possible, keep your hands shoulder-width apart. Hold for three to five minutes.

- When you are ready, begin to walk your arms back until you are resting on your haunches, head still on the floor. Take your arms back by your sides, hands pointing toward your feet. You are now resting in child's pose. Stay here for a few moments or for as long as you choose.

How to appreciate who you are

How often do you look at what is good within you?
Often, we move away from seeing the good within
ourselves in case we are seen as arrogant or boastful.
When we don't give space and time to appreciate
who we truly are, it allows criticism to creep in. This
Pause Practice takes the form of a letter that you
write to yourself, and is designed to reconnect you
compassionately to the good within you. Play some
music while writing it, if you like.

Pause with a letter of gratitude to yourself

Time 20–30 minutes
Frequency When you notice you are
being hard on yourself
Location Your favourite, inspiring place,
perhaps where you write your journal

Preparation

• You will need some writing paper, an envelope and a pen.

Exercise

• This letter is going to be one of deep appreciation and
gratitude for yourself. It is as though you are writing to
your best friend, with words full of love and compassion.
You will write about the strengths within you, the qualities
you have that you are most grateful for, the beauty that is
in you and the support you have around you.

• Start with "Dear" and insert your name. Begin writing
and don't stop until you have completed it and nothing
else needs to be said or expressed.

• When you are ready, read it back to yourself, out loud if
you want to. Then put your letter in the envelope and seal
it. Keep it in a safe place so you can come back to it at a
time when your heart needs to hear some kind words.

7

pause
for technology

How to break your smartphone addiction

Do you reach for your smartphone first thing in the morning? Are you constantly connected throughout the day, checking apps, messages, email, and social media in every spare moment? This has become such a normal way of life that you may not even consider it an addiction. After all, your smartphone connects you to your global family and friends, enables you to do business on the move, gets you to your destination on time, connects you to instant news, big ideas, and kindred spirits. Could you live without it? What would that even look like?

Even though this is still a new technology that did not exist before the turn of the new millennium, for most of us, the idea of living without a smartphone would now be unimaginable. Yet human beings were not designed to be always available. Healthy smartphone habits, if you can develop them, will allow you to stay connected to yourself and the world around you in the way that your heart desires.

This exercise, called electronic sundown (you can create others), is designed to help you begin to break your smartphone addiction.

Pause with electronic sundown

Time 2 minutes
Frequency Every evening for 7 days
Location Wherever you are

Preparation

• Decide on your watershed and buy an alarm clock.

Exercise

- This is a simple process that creates a watershed for smartphone usage. You decide what that watershed time is to be. For instance, it might be one hour before you go to bed. At that time each evening, put your smartphone on charge in the kitchen (or another room that is not your bedroom) and set it to airplane mode. The idea is to create a break between you and your phone where it is not in your presence.

- Set your alarm clock to wake you up in the morning so that there really is no need to have your smartphone in your bedroom overnight. This also minimizes the urge to switch it on when you wake up. Practise this for seven days and see what you discover!

How to keep FOMO in check

The fear of missing out (or FOMO) can creep up on any one of us in an instant – over coffee with a friend, seeing a colleague promoted, a conversation at the school gates – and social media often exacerbates it. Those glimpses into other people's lives online spark a fear inside, leaving you wondering: shouldn't your life be that glamorous, exciting, adventurous and fun?

FOMO is really a form of social anxiety, the worry that other people are happier, wealthier and more contented than you are. When you feel FOMO, it's likely that you have moved away from your own place, your own inner essence, and into someone else's world. Understand that and you will see that the way back from FOMO is to ground yourself in your own reality, rather than attempting to attain what others have.

This Pause Practice is designed to help you consider some questions that will help you become grounded in your own essence again.

Pause with your own reality

Time 10–20 minutes

Frequency Whenever you feel FOMO

Location Anywhere that you can write your journal

Preparation

• You will need your journal and a pen.

Exercise

• Ask yourself the following questions and write your answers in your journal.

• *BELIEF*
What do I believe about myself?
Where do I see myself as less than others?
Where do I see others as more than I am?
What is the truth?

• *TRUST*
What can I trust about me as a person?
What can I trust about where I currently am in life?
Who can I trust around me?
What examples do I have to show that I can trust life?

• *GROUNDING*
What are the guiding principles that matter most to me?
What are my personal values?
What do I most want from life?
How do I want to feel?

pause
for restful sleep

8

How to prepare for sleep

Most mothers with new babies instinctively know to create a regular rhythm for the newborns to help them settle. As adults in a fast-paced world, we experience fewer regular rhythms, often reacting to other's needs before our own, both at work and at home. This lack of rhythm can leave you feeling tired but wired when you go to bed at night, so you drop your head onto the pillow feeling exhausted, but your mind is wide-awake and racing. It can really help to create an evening ritual for yourself. This doesn't need to take a lot of time – just getting used to doing the same thing each evening will help your central nervous system settle before bedtime.

The following is a suggestion for an evening ritual, but you can create your own, one that works best for you. In any case, it's a good idea to set a time for bed and keep to it.

Pause with a bedtime ritual

Time 15 minutes before bedtime
Frequency Daily
Location At home

Preparation

- You will need some lavender essential oil, an oil burner, if you have one, or a diffuser, a journal and a pen.

Exercise

- Make sure your smartphone is switched to airplane mode and is on charge in another room (see Pause with electronic sundown, page 62). Locate your keys, purse or wallet and any travel cards you need for the following day. Put them in an accessible place.

- Complete all your usual bedtime activities and when they are finished, go to your bedroom, draw the curtains, if they are not already closed, and switch on a lamp (not the main light). If you have an oil burner or diffuser, add some lavender oil to it and switch it on now. You could light a candle as well.

- Find a place to sit and add three drops of lavender oil to the palms of your hands. Inhale deeply and exhale gently, repeating three times. As you inhale the lavender oil, let your shoulders begin to relax, loosen your jaw and notice how you feel in your body.

- As you let your body relax and soften, take your journal and make a note of anything you know is on your mind. Then write three things you feel grateful for today.

- Put your journal to one side and inhale the lavender oil three more times, allowing your body to relax each time you exhale.

- When you are ready, blow out any candles, sprinkle three drops of lavender oil on your pillow and turn off the lamp as you get into bed.

How to let go of what keeps you awake

Sometimes it can be hard to sleep because you have a lot of things weighing on your mind. If you find this happens on a few consecutive nights, it might be a good time to set up a fire ritual one evening, or at the weekend. Fire has the power to transform, create and purify. In ancient traditions, fire was held in reverence and infused with prayer and intention – these rituals continue in some countries today.

While this ritual won't eradicate the cause of your worries, creating your own fire ritual can be a supportive way of acknowledging, releasing and transforming the fears that keep you awake at night. If your mind is full, try the Pause Practice described on the follwing pages one evening and see if it helps you to sleep well and feel renewed and restored.

Pause with a fire ritual

Time 20–30 minutes
Frequency Occasionally, when you can't sleep.
You can also do this ritual on a new moon or a full moon
Location At home

Preparation

- There are two parts to the preparation. The first is to find a place where you can safely light a fire. If you have a hearth in your home or a fire pit in the garden, lay a fire ready to be lit. If you don't have a natural place for a fire, you could burn your paper over a candle. Just make sure that you have a safe place to let the flames burn out.

- The second part of the preparation is to write down all of your fears and worries on individual pieces of paper.

- As an option, you could have a smudging stick of white sage (*Salvia apiana*) or a Palo Santo stick to burn for additional cleansing and purification. (A smudging stick is a small bundle of dried herbs, tied together with string; a Palo Santo stick is an incense stick made from the *Bursera graveolens* tree, native to South and Central America.)

Exercise

- If you are using a smudging stick or Palo Santo, light this first and waft the smoke around the space where you are holding the ritual.

- Next, light your fire, or candle, and spend some time watching the flames as they rise.

- When you are ready, take your first piece of paper, read it (either out loud or to yourself) and in your own time place it on the fire or in the flame to burn. Watch the colours in the fire change, and notice how you feel in your body as the flames transform the paper to ash. Repeat until all the pieces of paper have been placed into the fire.

- Sit for a while and be aware of your body. Blow out the candle. If it is safe to do so, you can leave your fire to burn itself out. If it isn't safe to do this, make sure you put it out before you go to sleep.

9

pause
for inner peace

How to practise loving kindness

The ability to be loving and kind to others stems from being loving and kind to ourselves.

This Pause Practice involves you inwardly reciting a series of traditional phrases. The exercise is in two parts, firstly directing loving kindness to yourself and then to others. If other feelings, such as frustration, irritation or anger, arise, come back to being loving and kind toward yourself.

Pause with loving kindness meditation

————

Time 15–20 minutes
Frequency As often as you want
Location A quiet place

Preparation

• None

Exercise

• Sit in a comfortable position and let your body rest and
  be relaxed. Be aware of anything that is preoccupying
  your mind and consciously put that to one side. Allow
  your heart to open and soften. Breathe gently.

• Begin the meditation by directing the following phrases
  toward yourself and your own sense of well-being.
  Repeat the words over and over as you allow your heart
  to open and your body to be permeated by feelings of
  loving kindness.

- *May I be filled with loving kindness.*

- *May I be safe from inner and outer dangers.*

- *May I be well in body and mind.*

- *May I be at ease and happy.*

- After about ten minutes, expand your meditation to include another person. Choose someone who has loved or cared for you. Picture this person and then recite the same phrases:

- *May you be filled with loving kindness.*

- *May you be safe from inner and outer dangers.*

- *May you be well in body and mind.*

- *May you be at ease and happy.*

- Continue to allow your heart to open during this practice, sowing the seeds of love and kindness.

How to reconnect with your heart when you've been hurt

A natural response to heartbreak is to gather energetic protective layers around yourself to prevent further hurt and pain. Over time, if we don't open our hearts to love again, these layers can create cynicism or bitterness. The simple Pause Practice described on the following pages gently allows you to reconnect with your heart so you can come back to a natural loving state.

Pause with a healing heart meditation

Time 10 minutes
Frequency Whenever you want to be open to love
Location At home

Preparation

- Lay a yoga mat or blanket on the floor.

Exercise

- Lie on your back with your legs straight and slightly apart and your arms gently outstretched, palms facing upward. Close your eyes and take a few moments to arrive.

- Now inhale and on the exhale let go of any tension in your face. Inhale again and on the exhale let go of any tension in your shoulders. Continue breathing in and out, letting go of any tension in your stomach, legs and finally in your whole body.

- In this exercise, you are going to alter the regular journey of the breath through the body. On the next inhale, imagine the breath starting at your right hand and moving horizontally across your body, arriving at your heart. Now breathe in through your left hand, sending the breath across your body into your heart. Repeat five times.

- Now breathe directly into your heart and let the breath move up to your head. Repeat five times.

- Then breathe into your heart and let the breath move down to your feet. Repeat five times.

- Now place your hand on your heart and send the breath directly under your hand for five breaths.

- Keep your hand on your heart and take a moment to create a loving intention for yourself. Let this intention infuse your heart and your whole being.

- Gently place your hand back to the outstretched position and take a moment to feel the open space in your heart. Finish by turning on your side and curling up into a foetal position. This is a reminder that you can always protect yourself whenever you need to.

pause
for balance

10

How to ground yourself when you feel out of balance

This next simple exercise can be used regularly, every day if you want to. It takes just a few minutes. You can do it during your lunch break – outside if you can, sitting against a tree, on a roof terrace or on a park bench.

Pause with a grounding meditation

Time 10 minutes

Frequency Whenever you need to feel more grounded

Location A seat outside

Preparation

• None

Exercise

• Once you have found a place to sit, feel your feet on the ground, and let the back of the seat take your weight. If you want to take your shoes off, you can. This gives you extra grounding, especially if you have grass under your feet.

• Focus on your contact with the ground and the weight of your body on the seat. Soften your eyes so that you are not looking out at the world intensely. Bring your awareness to the pace and rhythm of your breath without changing anything.

• Now gently move your attention to what is around you. Become aware of the air on your skin. How does it feel? Is it damp or dry, warm or cool? Can you feel sunshine, or mist, or the movement of a breeze on your skin?

- Notice what you can hear. Are leaves rustling in the trees? Is there the chatter of children nearby? Perhaps you can hear the sound of traffic or an aeroplane? Let yourself feel what you feel, and hear what you hear.

- Now expand your attention as broadly as you can, out to the horizon or up into the sky. Keep your eyes soft and take a couple of breaths as you allow your attention to widen naturally without forcing it. If your mind is racing, keep feeling your feet on the ground and breathe gently as you allow your attention to open out.

- Let your shoulders drop and relax your jaw while gently extending your attention with each breath.

- When you are ready, shift your focus back to the area where you are sitting. Look at small details around you – grass or flowers growing, cracks in the pavement, the way the light moves and creates shadows.

- Keep your gaze soft and bring your awareness back to yourself on the seat. Feel grounded with your feet on the floor and your body making contact with the seat that supports you. Keep your gaze soft, come back to your natural rhythm of breathing and notice how you feel.

How to protect yourself from negative energy

Every day we are exposed to energy that is not our own. It comes from the seasons, people, advertising, weather, music, television, media, Wi-Fi and much more. We can't see this energy but we are sensitive to it, and sometimes it can disturb the balance of our own energy without us even realizing this has happened. That's why you might feel better when you leave the city and go to the ocean, where the energy is more soothing to the system.

Most people can't get to the beach every day, so this Pause Practice is designed to help protect you from negative energy. You can use it when you know you will be exposed to other people's energy, for example before you go to work or travel on the train or bus, or before seeing a particular person whom you find draining.

The practice is best done with your eyes closed, so don't try it while you're driving!

Pause with a light meditation

Time 3 minutes
Frequency Whenever you feel out of kilter with the world
Location A quiet place

Preparation

• None

Exercise

• Sit comfortably, feet flat on the ground. Let the chair support you. Close your eyes and wait for your breath to settle.

• Imagine a point of light about an inch from your nose. Allow it to travel over your chin and throat, keeping the same distance away.

• Imagine the light travelling across your chest from right to left, hovering over your heart to make sure this area is well protected.

• Let the light travel down your left arm, over your hand, underneath your palm and up to your armpit, back across your chest and down your right arm in the same way.

• Then imagine the light spreading across your entire torso, over your hips and down the front of your thighs, shins and feet.

Pause with light meditation (continued)

- Now let the light go beyond your feet and travel into the earth below – deep, deep, deeper down, right down into the core of the earth so you can draw the earth's energy directly from her source. Draw it up, up, allowing it to travel over the back of your heels, up your calves, thighs, over your hips, lower back and up your spine, pausing at the back of your neck to ensure this area is well protected. Allow the earth's energy to travel over the back of your head and rest for a moment at the crown before sending it to the heights of the heavens.

- Feel a golden light showering down from the skies softly infusing every cell of your body. It pours like golden liquid through your core and down through your feet back into the earth, drawing on her powerful core energy, billions and billions of years old.

- This majestic force covers your entire body and comes to rest at your third eye. Here is where you know the truth that you are fully protected and you have all the resources you need. The energy seals at the top of your head.

- Now imagine small psychic attacks coming toward you. Notice them bouncing off your energetic protection. Follow this with medium psychic attacks, which make no dent in your shield.

- Then call on four black unicorns, your final layer of defence. Place one in front of you, facing outward. Place a second to the right of you, a third to the left and the last one behind you, all facing outward. Take a moment to feel this energetic protection.

- Now breathe, gently wriggle your fingers and toes and come back to the here and now.

Pause is a practice...

Sometimes being busy is so normal that we don't
even notice we need some time for our mind to
connect with our heart or for our soul to arrive back
in our body.

Pause is about finding moments in the madness to
reconnect with ourselves again. This doesn't have
to be time-consuming or complicated. The practices
in this book offer you tools and processes to help you
press Pause, but sometimes all we need to do is take
a breath and look up at the sky. At other times, all we
need to do is hold the gaze of the person talking to us,
or simply savour the warmth of the mug of tea in our
hands. Sometimes all that is needed to Pause is this
breath, right here, right now. And then another.

Pause is a practice. It is the art of staying awake and being with yourself among the noise of others. Pause is the ability to find compassion for yourself and the people around you when all we are fed is fear. Pause is the trust that life is for you, not against you, and that there are always greater forces at work. Pause is your way of taking an intimate journey with yourself this lifetime, letting your life unfold to a destination unknown.

There are five journal prompts on the following pages to help you keep exploring your own Pause.

Five journal prompts to help you pause in everyday life

1 If you want to deepen your understanding of your path and purpose in life, use:

I went to the Master and asked, "Master what do I need to know?" and the Master said...

2 If you want to create clarity about what you need in your life, use:

What I want is... (go deep, expressing more than just the material aspects of your life)

3 If you are feeling stuck, and want to let go of the old to make way for the new, work with:

I choose to let go of... Followed by: *I choose to let in...*

4 If you are curious to find out what might be blocking you in life, especially if it feels hidden from you, use:

What don't I want to know about me / my life / my situation right now?

5 If you want to spend some time reflecting on and celebrating your life, use:

I am grateful for...

Journal tips

Once you have spent some time journaling, read back what you have written, or reflect on your artwork, and allow any insights to emerge.

Remember, you can fill your journal however, and in whatever way, you choose. Be creative and think about mixing it up sometimes. For example:

• **Journal with friends.** You don't have to be alone. You may find friends who would be happy to gather and journal together in the evenings or at the weekend.

- **Journal outside**. You don't always have to stay inside. Why not be inspired by nature – take your journal down into the woods, to the top of a hill or alongside a lake or stream.

- **Let go of what you express**. You don't always have to keep your journal entries. You might like to sit and write by the light of the fire and then create a ceremony to release the words into the flames.

- Finally, **don't try to force this** (or any part of the process). Like a good coffee, or a profound coaching session, insights can take time to percolate and often reveal themselves long after the exercise itself has been completed.

Acknowledgements

To Life,
Our endless teacher.
With gratitude.

If you are ready for a deeper Pause, visit
www.thepauseretreats.com